A Guide for Using

Where the Wild Things Are

in the Classroom

Based on the novel written by Maurice Sendak

*This guide written by **Susan Kilpatrick***

Teacher Created Resources, Inc.
6421 Industry Way
Westminster, CA 92683
www.teachercreated.com
©1994 Teacher Created Resources, Inc.
Reprinted, 2005
Made in U.S.A.
ISBN 1-55734-525-2

Illustrated by
Blanca Apodaca La Bounty

Cover Art by
Sue Fullam

Teacher Created Resources

Table of Contents

Introduction

A good book can touch the lives of children like a good friend. The pictures, words, and characters can inspire young minds as they turn to literary treasures for companionship, recreation, comfort, and guidance. Great care has been taken in selecting the books and unit activities that comprise the primary series of *Literature Units*. Teachers who use the literature unit to supplement their own valuable ideas can plan the activities using one of the following methods.

Sample Lesson Plan

The sample lessons on page 4 provide you with a specific set of lesson plan suggestions. Each of the lessons can take from one to several days to complete and can include all or some of the suggested activities. Refer to the "Suggestions for Using the Unit Activities" on pages 7-10 for information relating to the unit activities.

Unit Planner

If you wish to tailor the suggestions on pages 7-10 in a format other than that prescribed in the "Sample Lesson Plan," a blank unit planner is provided on page 5. On a specific day you may choose the activities you wish to include by writing the activity number or a brief notation about the lesson in the "Unit Activities" section. Space has been provided for reminders, comments, and other pertinent information relating to each day's activities. Reproduce copies of the "Unit Planner" as needed.

Sample Lesson Plan

Lesson 1

- Introduce the book by using some or all of the unit activities. (pages 7-10)
- Read "Getting to Know the Book and Author." (page 6)
- Discuss the new vocabulary with students. (page 7)
- Discuss the "big ideas." (page 7)
- Record responses on the left side of the "Knowledge Chart: What I Already Know About Monsters." (page 17)
- Read the story for enjoyment.
- Complete the right side of the "Knowledge Chart: What I Learned About Monsters." (page 17)

Lesson 2

- Read the story a second time.
- Prepare pocket chart and use the Bloom's Taxonomy cards and activities to involve students in critical thinking. (pages 11-14)
- Use the "Story Summary Sentence Strips." (pages 15-16)
- Recite poem: "Max Was a Wild Thing." (page 18)
- Complete "Character Minds" activity. (page 23)
- Follow directions to "Make a Monster." (pages 30-31)

Lesson 3

- Construct and write about scenes from "Where the Wild Things Are." (pages 21-22)
- Construct "Wild Things" booklets. (pages 25-26)
- Conduct "Sink or Float" experiment. (page 41)
- Begin practicing "Reader's Theater." (pages 45-46)

- Learn song "The King of the Wild Things." (page 43)

Lesson 4

- Complete the "Story Ladder." (page 24)
- Help students to distinguish between real and make-believe. (pages 27-28)
- Complete a picture Venn diagram comparing Max and a wild thing. (page 29)
- Involve students with drama using stick puppets. (pages 19-20)
- Talk about "Animal Coverings" and make a class chart. (page 40)
- Practice "Reader's Theater." (pages 45-46)

Lesson 5

- Discuss modes of transportation and complete "Ways to Travel" charts. (page 34)
- Construct "Wild Thing" puzzles. (page 38)
- Play "Copycat" game at P.E. time. (page 39)
- Complete "Cause and Effect" activity. (page 33)
- Practice "Reader's Theater." (pages 45-46)
- Practice poem and song. (pages 18 and 43)

Lesson 6

- Discuss "Needs and Wants" and make class booklet. (page 35)
- Complete "Sponge Painting" art (pages 36-37) and display on a bulletin board.
- Write "Gold Crown" stories (page 32) and display on a bulletin board.
- Prepare recipes on page 42. Serve foods after "Reader's Theater" presentation.
- Present "Reader's Theater," poem, and song as a culminating activity. See page 44 for suggestions.

Unit Planner

Date:	Unit Activities
Notes/Comments:	

Date:	Unit Activities
Notes/Comments:	

Date:	Unit Activities
Notes/Comments:	

Date:	Unit Activities
Notes/Comments:	

Date:	Unit Activities
Notes/Comments:	

Date:	Unit Activities
Notes/Comments:	

Getting to Know . . .

. . . the Book

(*Where the Wild Things Are* is published in the U.S. by HarperCollins. It is also available in Canada and AUS from HarperCollins and in the UK from Penguin.)

Max gets into so much mischief that he is sent to bed without his supper. Max imagines that a forest grows in his room, and he sails off in his own private boat to the land of the wild things. He tames the creatures with a magic trick, becomes their king, and leads them in a wild rumpus. When he starts to feel lonely, Max decides to sail back home to his own world where the people he loves—and a hot supper—are waiting for him.

. . . the Author

Author and illustrator Maurice Sendak was born in Brooklyn, New York. He wanted to write and illustrate from the time he was a young boy, and he has illustrated comic strips and designed sets and costumes for stage and film. His special talent is in remembering events other people do not recall—the sounds and feelings of childhood. He is credited with being the first artist to deal openly with the true feelings of young children. He won the Caldecott Award for his delightful book, *Where the Wild Things Are.*

6

Suggestions for Using the Unit Activities

Use some or all of the following suggestions to introduce students to *Where the Wild Things Are* and to extend their appreciation of the book through activities that cross the curriculum.

1. Use *Where the Wild Things Are* along with other stories to comprise a unit on monsters. (See Bibliography, page 48.) The following themes can be explored with *Where the Wild Things Are:*
   - real or make-believe
   - accepting consequences for one's behavior
   - the difference between having fun and making mischief
   - feelings

2. Before you begin the unit, prepare the monster-shaped vocabulary cards, story question sailboat cards, and the sentence strips for the pocket chart activities. (See samples, patterns, and directions on pages 11-16.)

3. Engage prior knowledge and oral language skills by asking the children to recall everything they already know about monsters. Record responses on the left side of the "Knowledge Chart" (page 17) under "What I Already Know About Monsters." (Record new knowledge on the right side of the chart after reading the story.)

4. Discuss the meanings of the following words in context before reading the story. Write the words on the monster-shaped task cards on page 13. Display words on a pocket chart. (See page 11 for directions on making a pocket chart.)
   - private
   - mischief
   - gnashed
   - supper
   - tamed
   - wild rumpus
   - terrible
   - tumbled
   - vines

5. Provide exposure to the following "big ideas":
   - Is an imagination a good thing to have?
   - Should we be kind to animals? (Max chased the dog with a fork.)
   - Should we talk back to our parents?
   - Are monsters real or make-believe?
   - Do we have to accept the consequences of our actions?
   - Is it okay to be angry, sad, and scared, as well as happy?

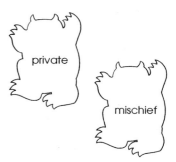

6. Display the book cover. Ask if the book will be about something real or a make-believe story.

7. Ask students to listen for new ideas about monsters. Read the story aloud for enjoyment and to discover new information about monsters. Record this new information on the "Knowledge Chart" under "What I Learned About Monsters."

Suggestions for Using the Unit Activities *(cont.)*

8. Develop critical thinking skills with the questions on page 14. The questions are based on Bloom's Taxonomy and are provided in each of Bloom's Levels of Learning. Use the sailboats to write out the story questions on page 14. Refer to pages 12 and 14 for information on how to use the "Story Question Sailboats."

9. Refer to the story sentences on pages 15-16 to prepare "Story Summary Sentence Strips." Laminate a set of sentences to use with a pocket chart. Work with students on some or all of the following activities:
    - On the pocket chart, sequence the sentences in the order in which the events happened in the story.
    - Use the sentences to retell the story.
    - Divide the class into small groups and distribute a few sentences to each group. Ask the groups to act out the parts of the story represented by their sentences.
    - In addition to these activities, you may wish to reproduce the sentence strips pages and have students read the sentences aloud to a partner or take them home to read to a parent or older sibling.

10. Reproduce "Max Was a Wild Thing" on page 18. Divide the class into six groups and assign each group a verse of the poem. Have the groups choral read and act out their verses.

11. Prepare "Stick Puppet Theaters" following the directions and suggestions on pages 19 and 20. Allow students to construct puppets by coloring, cutting, and gluing puppets on tongue depressors.

12. Have students construct a scene from *Where the Wild Things Are* and write about some of the events in the story. Directions, patterns, and sentence blocks are provided on pages 21-22.

13. Help students learn to put themselves in another person's place with the "Character Minds" activity on page 23. To prepare children for this activity, discuss several situations orally: "What might a teacher or a parent think if a child acts up? Behaves well?" "What might a child think when getting up to speak in front of the class? When getting ready to bat? When starting to take a test?" etc. Then work cooperatively to come up with some ideas that might have been in Max's mind, in his mother's mind, and in a wild thing's mind before completing the activity on page 23.

14. Use the "Story Ladder" activity on page 24 to help students sequence major story events.

15. Students can make a "Wild Things Booklet" (pages 25-26) to read to a partner and/or grownup. There are two sets of directions—one for younger students and one for older students.

16. Help students distinguish between real and make-believe situations. Provide each student with two 3" x 5" (7.5 cm x 12.5 cm) index cards, one with the word "real" written on it and the other labeled "make-believe." If possible, use two different colored index cards and laminate them for durability. Read several statements, some real and some make-believe, and ask students to hold up the appropriate card after each statement is read. Reproduce pages 27 and 28. Have students complete the "Real or Make-Believe?" activity by cutting out the word/phrase boxes on page 28 and pasting each box under the correct heading on page 27.

Suggestions for Using the Unit Activities *(cont.)*

17. Use a Venn diagram to compare Max and a wild thing. Have students complete "Alike and Different" on page 29 by writing in the appropriate areas how the two are alike and different. Young students can do this orally or at the chalkboard guided by the teacher. Older students can write responses, work cooperatively with a partner, or work together with the teacher as a class project. A complete Venn diagram might look like this:

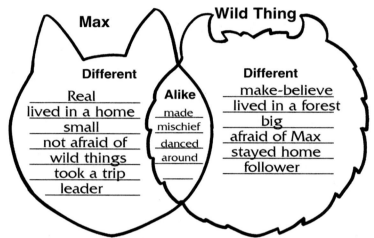

18. Reinforce the valuable skill of following directions with the "Make a Monster" activity on page 30. Two sets of directions are provided—one for younger students and one for older students.

19. Reproduce the "Gold Crown Story" activity on page 32. Motivate the writing process. Allow students to write a first draft, help them edit their papers, and then instruct them to complete their final copies on the gold crown. Display on a bulletin board with the wild things stencil sponge paintings under the heading "I'm in the Land of the Wild Things."

20. Orally, give students several situations (causes) and ask them to tell you what might happen in these instances (effects). Then ask them to complete the "Cause and Effect" paper on page 33. (This involves critical thinking.)

21. Max sailed away in a boat, but there are many other "Ways to Travel." See complete directions on page 34.

22. There is a big difference between "Needs and Wants." Help students understand this concept as they complete the activity on page 35.

23. You will love the results of "Sponge Painting." Follow directions on page 36 to make a set of four wild things stencils. Set up a paint center and have students sponge paint their monsters. Later when dry, they can select scary faces to complete their monsters.

24. Color a "Wild Thing Puzzle," cut it apart, and glue it back together. It is harder than you might think. This activity involves small motor coordination and completing one sentence which can be read aloud. See page 38.

Suggestions for Using the Unit Activities *(cont.)*

25. A great indoor or outdoor physical activity, "Copycat" combines movement and chanting with exercising memory. See complete directions on page 39 and have fun with this one.

26. The "Animal Coverings" activity on page 40 contains a chart which can be used to classify animals according to their "skins" or coverings.

27. "Sink or Float" on page 41 is based on Max's boat which floated on the ocean. Students predict whether various objects will sink or float in a tub of water.

28. Use the "Wild Things Recipes" suggestions on page 42 to prepare "Tuna Boats" and "Wild Thing Cookies."

29. Culminating Activity

    Use the "Reader's Theater Script" on pages 45–46 to involve students in a dramatic interpretation of the book.

    Following the "Reader's Theater Script," have students recite the poem on page 18, "Max Was a Wild Thing" by S. Kilpatrick and sing the song on page 43, "The King of the Wild Things" by M.E. Hicks.

    Prepare for and practice the script well before the end of the unit. You may wish to invite other classes and parents to see the programs and enjoy the music. (See "An Invitation to a Wild Rumpus" on page 47.) Display related art and writing projects. This would also be a good time to serve the dishes described on page 42.

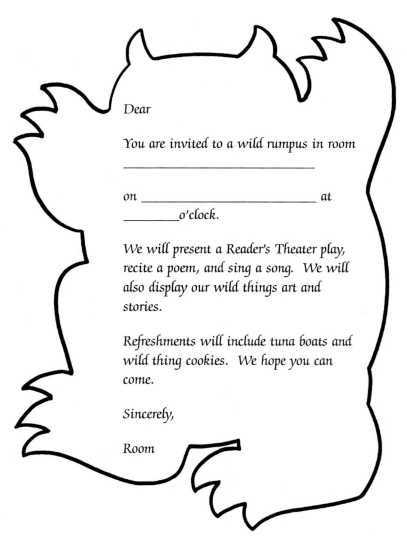

Dear

You are invited to a wild rumpus in room

_____

on _____ at _____o'clock.

We will present a Reader's Theater play, recite a poem, and sing a song. We will also display our wild things art and stories.

Refreshments will include tuna boats and wild thing cookies. We hope you can come.

Sincerely,

Room

Pocket Chart Activities

A pocket chart can be used to hold the vocabulary cards (wild things shape), the Bloom's Taxonomy questions cards (sailboat shape), and the sentence strips.

How to Make a Pocket Chart

If a commercial pocket chart is unavailable, you can make a pocket chart if you have access to a laminator. Begin by laminating a 24" x 36" (60 cm x 90 cm) piece of colored tagboard. Run about 20" (50 cm) of additional plastic. To make nine pockets, cut the clear plastic into nine equal strips. Space the strips equally down the 36" (90 cm) length of the tagboard. Attach each strip with cellophane tape along the bottom and sides. This will hold sentence strips, word cards, etc., and can be displayed in a learning center or mounted on a chalk tray for use with a group. When your pocket chart is ready, use it to display the sentence strips, vocabulary words, and question cards. A sample chart is provided below.

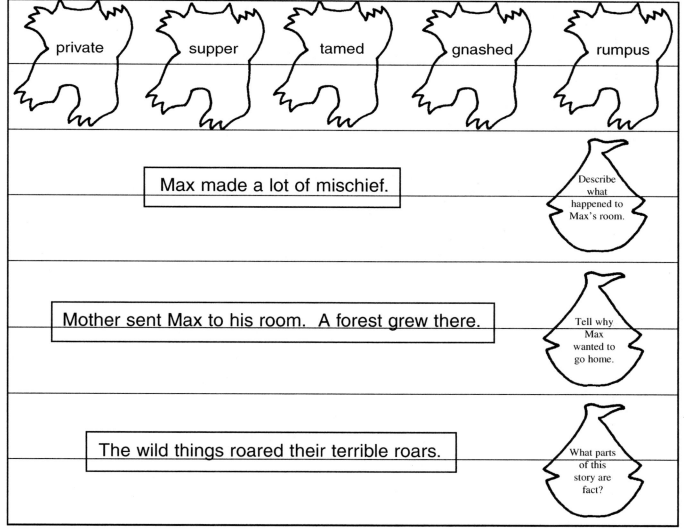

Pocket Chart Activities *(cont.)*

How to Use the Pocket Chart

---

1. Present the wild thing vocabulary cards before reading the book to familiarize students with difficult words and their meanings. Help students understand the word meanings by giving them context clues.

2. Reproduce several copies of the boat pattern (page 13) on colored construction paper. Use one color for each level of Bloom's Levels of Learning.

For example:

   I.   Knowledge (green)

   II.   Comprehension (pink)

   III.   Application (lavender)

   IV.   Analysis (orange)

   V.   Synthesis (blue)

   VI.   Evaluation (yellow)

Describe what happened to Max's room.

Tell why Max wanted to go home.

Write a question from page 14 on the appropriate color-coded sailboat. Write the level of the question on the sail. Write the question on the hull of the sailboat. Laminate the sailboat for durability.

Use the sailboat-shaped cards after the story has been read to develop and practice higher-level critical thinking skills by using the color-coded sailboats with some or all of the following activities:

- Use the cards to question a group or the class.
- Have students "draw" a card, read aloud, or give to teacher to read aloud. Student answers the question or calls on another student to answer the question.
- Students are paired together. Teacher reads a question. Students take turns telling each other the answers (or giving opinions).
- Play a game: Divide group into teams. Score a point for a correct (or a reasonable) answer.
- Mix up cards from several different stories. Students or teams must name the story and answer the question.
- Have cross-age tutors read the story and use question cards.

3. Use the sentence strips to practice oral reading and sequencing of the story events. Reproduce pages 15-16. If possible, laminate for durability. Cut out the sentence strips or prepare sentences of your own to use with the pocket chart.

He sailed home to his very own room.

The wild things made Max their king.

Pocket Chart Patterns

See page 12 for directions.

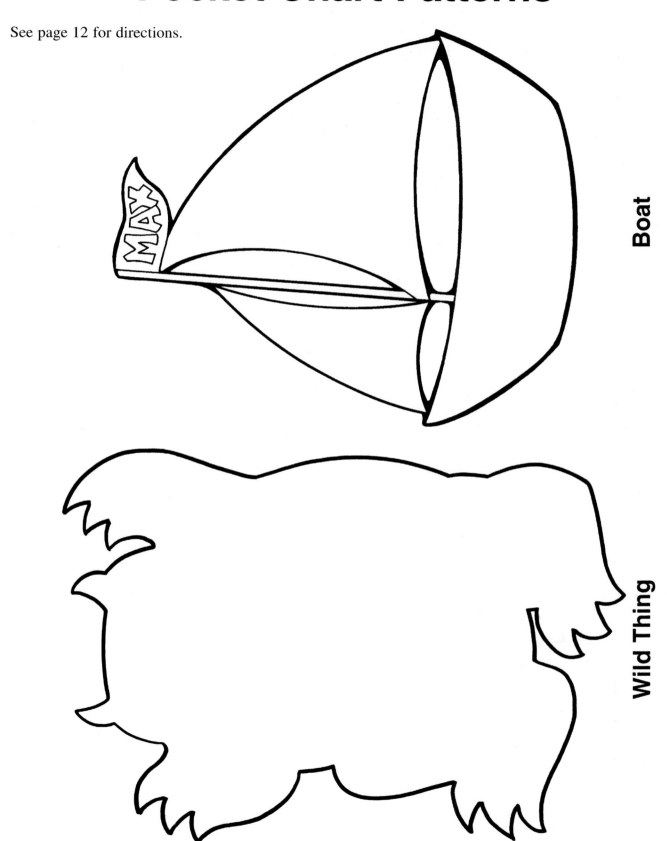

Boat

Wild Thing

Story Question Sailboats

The following questions are based on Bloom's Taxonomy.

Use the following questions with the activities on page 12. Using the sailboats made from the sailboat pattern on page 13, copy one question per sailboat.

I. Knowledge (ability to recall learned information)

- What did Max wear while he was making mischief?
- Why did Max's mother call him a "wild thing"?
- Describe what happened to Max's room.
- What did the wild things do? (with their teeth, their eyes, their claws)

II. Comprehension (basic understanding of information)

- Tell why Max wanted to go home.
- Explain how Max became king of the wild things.
- Who do you think put Max's supper in his room? Why do you think it was placed there?

III. Application (ability to do something new with information)

- If Max had not yelled at his mother, "I'll eat you up!" what might have happened?
- What might have happened if Max had been afraid of the wild things?

IV. Analysis (ability to examine the parts of a whole)

- What parts of this story are fact? (true)
- What parts of this story are fiction? (not true)

V. Synthesis (ability to bring together information to make something new)

- Make up a different way for Max to get to the place where the wild things are found.
- What else could Max have done with the wild things? What would you have done?
- How else could this story have ended?

VI. Evaluation (ability to form and defend an opinion)

- Do you think the wild things loved Max?
- Does Max have a good imagination? Why or why not?
- What kind of a mother do you think Max has? Why?
- If you were Max's mother, how would you have punished him? (instead of sending him to his room with no dinner)

Story Summary Sentence Strips

See page 8 (activity 9) for directions.

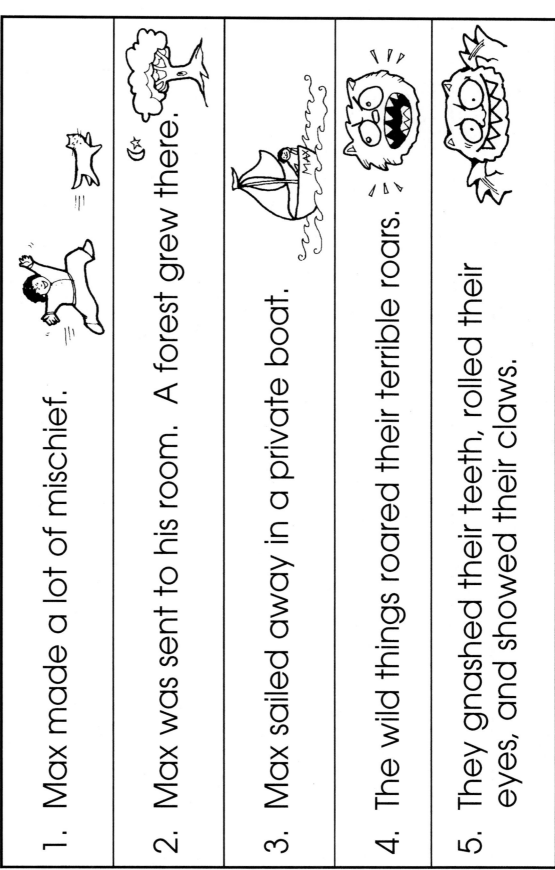

1. Max made a lot of mischief.

2. Max was sent to his room. A forest grew there.

3. Max sailed away in a private boat.

4. The wild things roared their terrible roars.

5. They gnashed their teeth, rolled their eyes, and showed their claws.

Story Summary Sentence Strips *(cont.)*

See page 8 (activity 9) for directions.

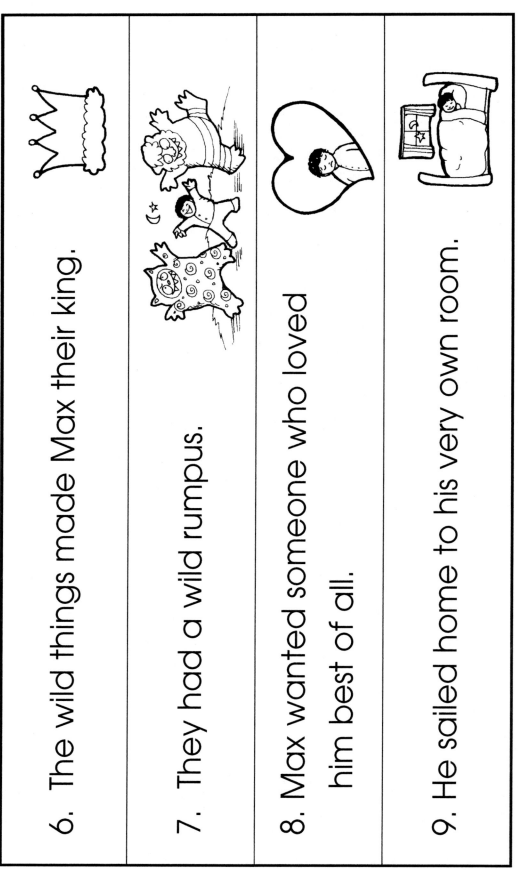

6. The wild things made Max their king.

7. They had a wild rumpus.

8. Max wanted someone who loved him best of all.

9. He sailed home to his very own room.

Suggestions to the Teacher: 1. Print sentences on sentence strips for use in a pocket chart. 2. Duplicate pages 15 and 16. Have students read them aloud to a partner and/or take them home to read to a parent.

Knowledge Chart

(Fill in before reading story.)

(Fill in after reading story.)

What I Already Know About Monsters	What I Learned About Monsters
1.	1.
2.	2.
3.	3.
4.	4.
5.	5.
6.	6.
7.	7.

Max Was a Wild Thing

Max was a wild thing,
He liked to yell and scream.
He sailed off through night and day;
Was it real or just a dream?

Max met some wild things,
He listened to them roar.
They gnashed their teeth and rolled their eyes,
They walked along the shore.

Max used a magic trick
To tame each scary beast,
They crowned him their new King, and
He said, "We'll have a feast."

Max cried out to everyone,
(He wore his new gold crown),
"Let the wild rumpus start,
Let's dance and march around!"

Then Max said, "It's time for me
To sail the ocean blue.
I miss my home and family,
So long to each of you."

The wild things called, "We love you!"
"Don't leave us, Max, please stay!"
But Max said, "No!" and off he sailed
Over a year and through a day.

— By Susan Kilpatrick

Stick Puppet Theaters

Make a class set of puppet theaters (one for each student) or make one theater for every 2-4 students.

Materials:

- 22" x 28" (56 cm x 71 cm) pieces of colored poster board (enough for each student or group of students)
- colored markers, crayons, or paints
- craft knife or scissors

Directions:

1. Cut a piece of colored poster board in half. (Makes two).
2. Fold sides back.
3. Cut a "window" in the front panel.
4. Let students personalize and decorate their own theater fronts. (Send them home at the end of the year or save to use year after year.)

Stick Puppet Theaters *(cont.)*

Suggestions for using the puppets and puppet theaters:

- Use the puppets and the puppet theaters with the Reader's Theater script on pages 45-46. (Have small groups of students take turns reading the parts and using the stick figures.)

- Let students experiment with the puppets while telling the story in their own words or reading from the book.

- As you make statements about the characters in the book, students can hold up the correct stick puppets. Read each statement below and have students hold up the stick puppet that represents who or what might have said it.

"WILD THING!"

(Max's mother)

"Let the wild rumpus start!"

(Max)

"Oh please don't go—we'll eat you up—we love you so!"

(wild things)

Story Scenes from
Where the Wild Things Are

Directions:

Give each student a large sheet of white construction paper or butcher paper.

Have students draw Max's room, as shown in the illustration to the right. You may wish to draw these on the chalkboard and have your students copy them on their pictures.

Reproduce and hand out a copy of the "Sentence Blocks" on page 22 to each student. Help students use the listed words at the top in sentences that relate the block title to the story. If age appropriate, reinforce the use of capitals, periods, quotations, commas in a series, contractions, possessives, etc.

Have students cut out and glue the sentence blocks to their pictures. It is not necessary to place the sentence blocks in a specific order.

A set of sentence blocks might look like this:

1. Bed	**2. Forest**
Max got sent to bed without supper.	A forest grew in Max's bedroom.

3. Ocean	**4. Wild Things**
Max sailed on the ocean for a long time.	The wild things tried to scare Max by showing their teeth and claws.

5. King	**6. Supper**
Max became king of the wild things.	Max's supper was waiting for him when he returned from his trip.

Sentence Blocks

Directions: Use with the "Story Scenes from *Where the Wild Things Are*" activity on page 21.

1. Bed

2. Forest

3. Ocean

4. Wild Things

5. King

6. Supper

Character Minds

Directions: After reading *Where the Wild Things Are*, write in the space provided below what you think each character (Max, Max's mother, one of the wild things) is thinking.

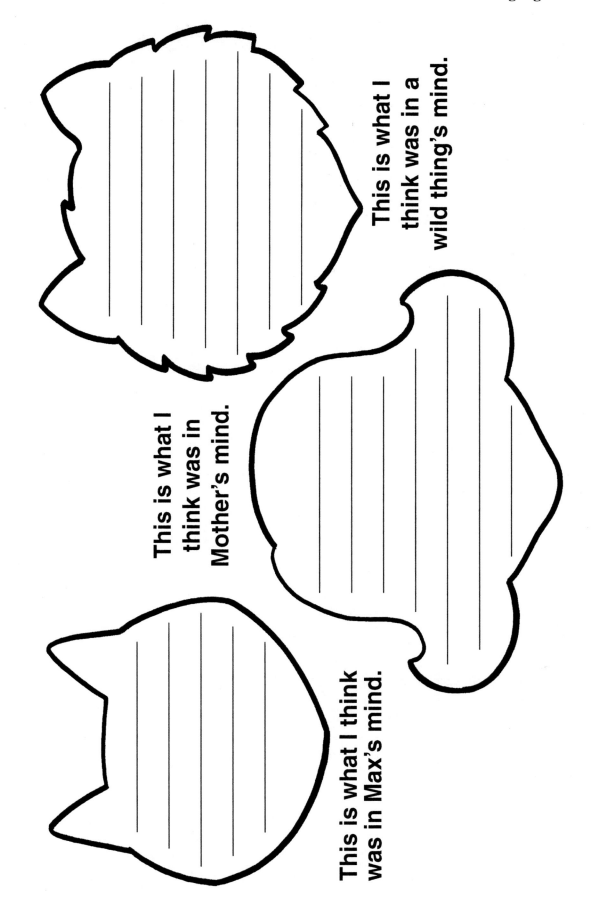

This is what I think was in a wild thing's mind.

This is what I think was in Mother's mind.

This is what I think was in Max's mind.

Story Ladder

Directions: Reproduce this page so each student can have a copy. Then have students cut out all five sentence blocks and arrange them on the story ladder in the order they took place in the story. Once the sentence blocks are in the correct order, students can either glue or tape the sentence blocks to the story ladder.

A forest grew in his room. There were trees and vines.

Max sailed home and found a hot dinner waiting.

Max made mischief and was sent to his room.

He became king, and they all had a wild rumpus.

Max sailed away to where the wild things are.

Name: _____

Title: _____

Author: _____

Story Ladder

	5
	4
	3
	2
	1

Wild Things Booklet

Materials:

- 2 or 3 copies of page 26 per student
- two sheets of colored construction paper per student
- scissors
- colored markers or crayons
- copy of directions

Directions: *(Younger Students)* four pages

Have students copy sentences from the chalkboard onto their booklet pages, one sentence per page of their booklets. After each sentence has been copied, have students illustrate that page to match what the sentence says. Then, when students have finished their booklets, have them read their stories to a grownup and/or student partner.

Sample Sentences:

1. Wild things gnash their teeth.
2. Wild things show their claws.
3. Wild things roll their eyes.
4. Wild things swing from trees.

Directions: *(Older Students)* five pages

Either students and teacher or cooperative groups of students can work together to compose five sequential sentences that tell a story. One sentence should go on each page of a student booklet. When the sentences have been written, have students illustrate their pages to match their stories. Then, when students have finished their booklets, have them read their stories to a grownup and/or student partner.

Sample Sentences:

1. Max wore his wolf suit and made mischief.
2. Mother said, "Wild Thing! Go to bed without dinner!"
3. That night, a forest grew in Max's room.
4. Max sailed away in his very own private boat.
5. Max went to the place where the wild things were.

Note to the Teacher: Talk about quotation marks, possessives, capitals, periods, etc., as students compose their sentences.

Wild Things Booklet *(cont.)*

Where the Wild Things Are

by Maurice Sendak

Where the Wild Things Are

by Maurice Sendak

Real or Make-Believe?

Directions: Read the words/phrases on page 28. Cut them out and glue under the correct heading.

Make-Believe

Real

Real or Make-Believe? *(cont.)*

Directions: Read each words/phrases, cut out, and glue under the correct heading.

a wolf	an elf	water	teeth
claws	a pink cat	a forest	a giant
a dragon monster	a flying dog	a bed	

Alike and Different

Directions: In the pictures, write your ideas of how Max and the wild things are alike and how they are different.

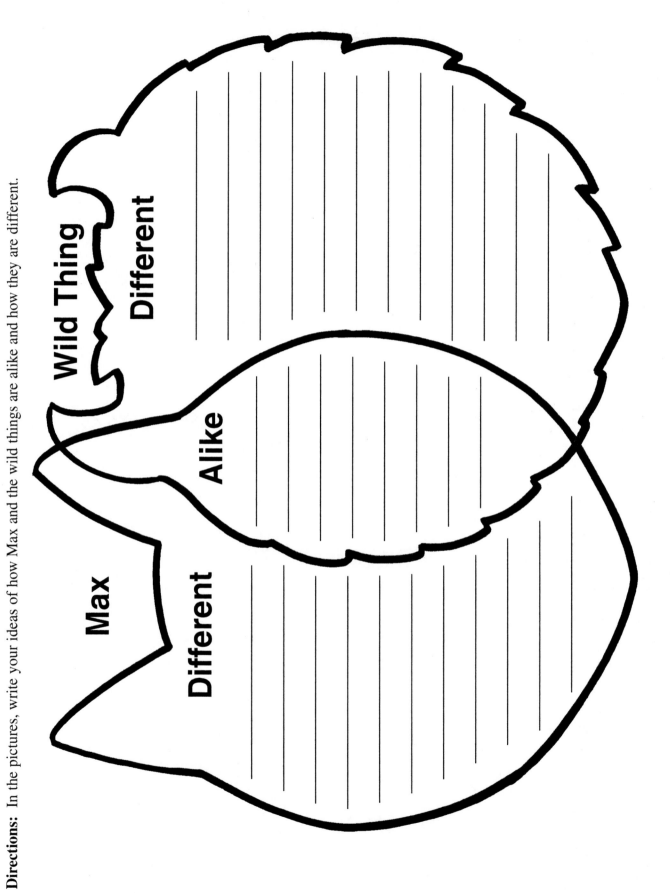

Wild Thing

Different

Alike

Max

Different

Make a Monster

Materials:

- one large piece of colored construction paper per student
- colored markers or crayons
- copy of monster (page 31), one per student
- glue or tape
- copy of directions

Directions: *(Younger Students)*

On the monster shape, draw:

1. three purple eyes
2. a mouth with two red teeth
3. orange hair on its head
4. brown ears
5. yellow spots
6. a blue tail
7. green claws
8. a black nose

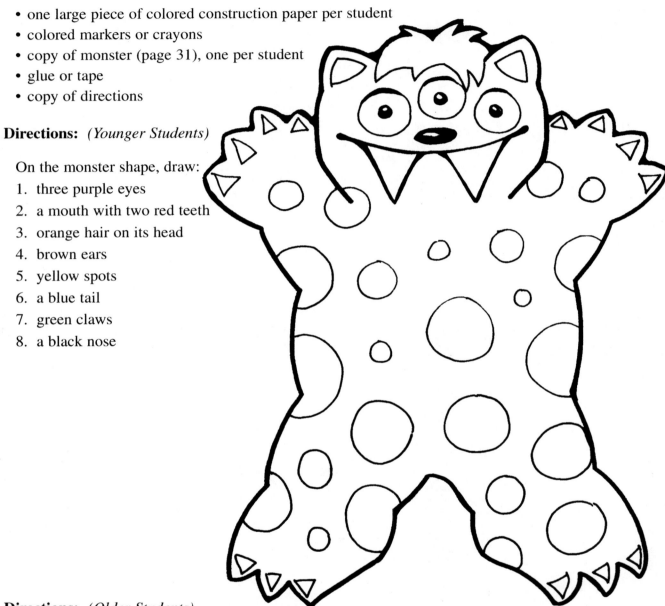

Directions: *(Older Students)*

1. On the monster shape, draw three purple eyes, a mouth with two red teeth, and a black nose.
2. Put some orange hair on the monster's head.
3. Give it some brown ears and a blue and red striped tail.
4. Draw some green claws for its hands.
5. Make purple and yellow spots on its body.
6. Draw a tiny mouse in the corner.
7. Draw yourself with a balloon in your hand standing next to the monster.

Make a Monster *(cont.)*

See page 30 for directions.

Gold Crown Story

Directions: Write a story about the following sentence: What would you do if the wild things made you their king or queen?

Start your story this way: If I were King (Queen) of the Wild Things, I would . . .

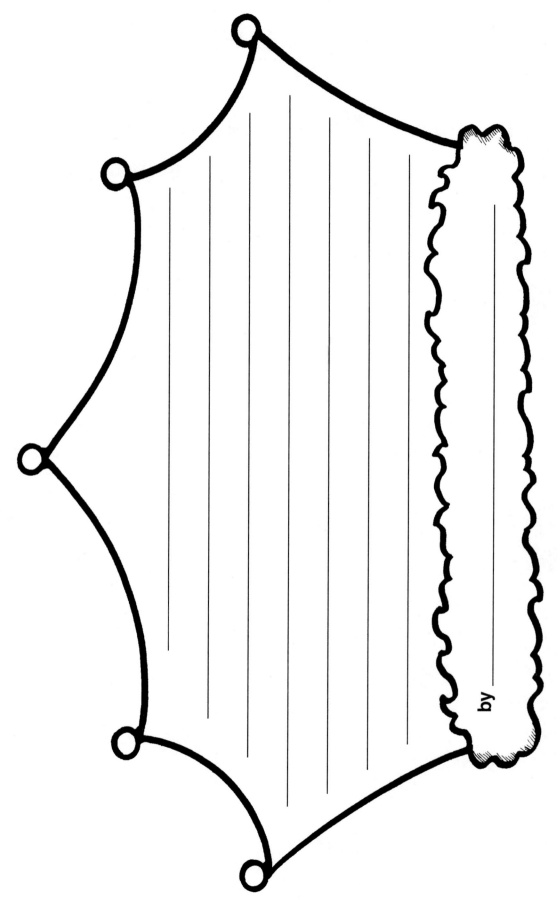

by _____

Cause and Effect

Directions: The "cause" is given. Write a possible "effect" for each.

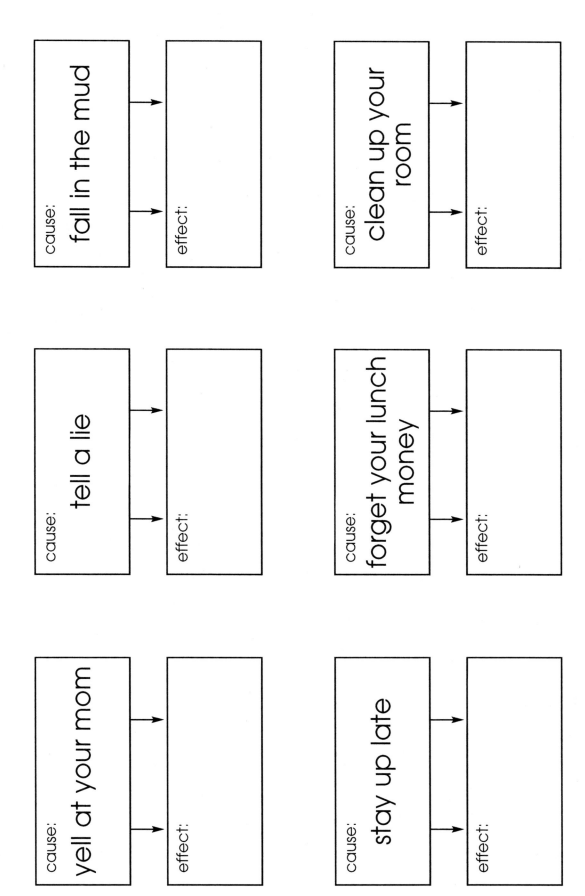

cause:
fall in the mud

effect:

cause:
tell a lie

effect:

cause:
yell at your mom

effect:

cause:
clean up your room

effect:

cause:
forget your lunch money

effect:

cause:
stay up late

effect:

Ways to Travel

1. Remind students that Max traveled by boat and Pete (in the "Reader's Theater Script") traveled by hot air balloon.

2. Ask students why people have invented various modes of transportation over the years.

3. Have students form groups and make a list of as many modes of transportation as possible. Then have the groups come together and share their ideas to make a master list.

4. Have each student fold a piece of white construction paper into eight sections.

1	2	3	4
5	6	7	8

5. Have students write "Ways to Travel" in their first block and in the remaining seven blocks, write different ways to travel. After coming up with seven different ways, illustrate them and share them with the class.

Needs and Wants

Directions:

1. Have students brainstorm a list of items they would need if they were to set out on a boat like Max did. Each student should come up with at least ten items.

2. After students come up with a list of things they would need, have them come up with a list of items they would want to take.

3. When both lists are finished, tell students they are going on a boat trip and can take only ten items. Have students make a list of what they take.

4. Attach each student's list to a piece of construction paper and have students illustrate their papers.

5. Collect all of the students' pages and create a class booklet that can be displayed for everyone to see.

Sponge Painting

Materials:

- scissors
- large piece of poster board or tagboard
- sponges (cut into different shapes)
- tempera (variety of colors)
- white construction paper, one piece per student
- pen or pencil
- glue
- copy of monster faces
- copy of wild thing shape (page 37)

Directions:

1. Divide and cut posterboard or tagboard into four pieces.

2. Cut out and glue the wild thing shape on each of the four pieces of posterboard or tagboard. Then, cut out the wild thing shape to make four stencils.

3. Have students share the stencils as they trace the wild thing shape onto their construction paper.

4. After shapes have been traced, have students sponge paint their pictures.

5. Next, have students either choose a monster face already drawn or make one themselves. They should color it and then glue it to their wild thing painting.

6. Students can create background scenes around their wild thing paintings if they desire.

- -

Sponge Painting *(cont.)*

Wild Thing Puzzle

Materials:

- colored markers or crayons
- scissors
- colored construction paper
- glue

Directions:

1. Draw and color a picture of a wild thing onto the puzzle pieces.

2. Carefully cut out the puzzle pieces on the dark lines.

3. Have a partner mix up your puzzle pieces.

4. Put your puzzle back together and glue it to a piece of colored construction paper.

5. Finish the sentence below. Choose an idea from the book or create an idea of your own.

6. Cut out the sentence block and glue it under your puzzle. Read the sentence aloud in class.

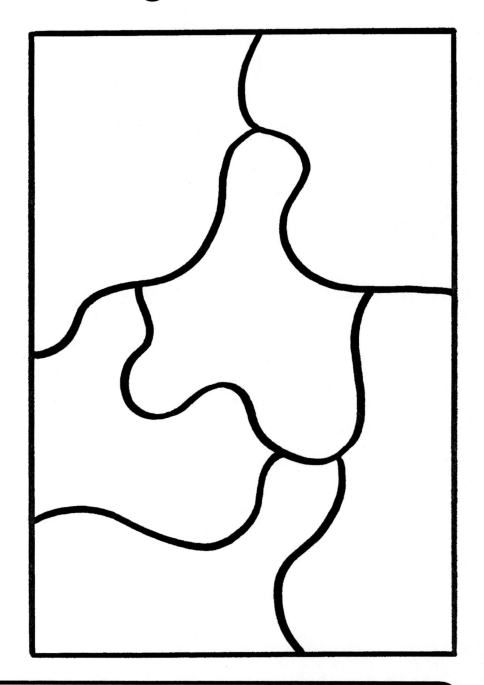

My wild thing likes to . . . _____

_____

_____

_____

Copycat

Directions:

1. Students sit or stand in a circle.

2. Teacher asks everyone to pretend to be a wild thing and think of an action to show the rest of the group.

3. Group says, "I am a wild thing. I like to jump up and down."
   (Teacher points to a student who adds an action. All students perform the action as they say the chant.)

4. Group repeats, "I am a wild thing. I like to jump up and down and snap my fingers."
   (Teacher points to a second student who adds another action. Students say the chant and perform the actions.)

5. Group repeats, "I am a wild thing. I like to jump up and down, snap my fingers, and turn around."
   (Teacher points to a third student who adds the next action. Students say the chant and perform the actions.)

Note to the Teacher: Continue as long as you like. See how many actions students can add and repeat in the correct order.

Animal Coverings

Animals may be covered by a variety of things. The type of covering an animal has will give you a hint as to what type of animal it is.

Materials:

- pen or pencil
- blank piece of paper, one per student

Directions:

1. Draw a chart on the chalkboard or on chart paper. Look at the example below to draw the chart. Have students copy the chart when it is completed.

Fur or Hair	Feathers	Scales	Skin	Plates or Shells
wild thing	penguin	fish	frog	turtle
zebra	eagle	snake	toad	lobster
hamster	canary	lizard	salamander	clam

2. Name various animals or hold up pictures of different animals. Ask students to classify them according to the chart above.

3. Write the names of the animals under the correct headings.

Sink or Float

Max's boat sailed off across the ocean. It did not sink; it floated.

Materials:

- tub
- water
- pen or pencil
- blank paper, one per student
- objects to test (apple, button, cork, craft stick, orange, paper clip, pencil, piece of chalk, scissors, etc.)

Directions:

1. Fill a tub with water.
2. Collect several objects.
3. Make a chart on the blackboard.
4. Have students copy the chart from the blackboard onto their blank papers.
5. Have students predict whether or not the objects will float. Then test each item in the water, and have them record what happens on their charts.

Sink	Float

Wild Things Recipes

Have a Wild Things Feast! Here are some creative dishes for you and your students to make and eat.

Max's Sailboat

1. Mix tuna and mayonnaise.
2. Spread on lightly toasted English muffins.
3. Slice cheese squares diagonally and weave a toothpick through each piece. Insert in muffin boats as shown.

Wild Things Cookies

1. Buy large, flat cookies—chocolate chip, oatmeal, sugar, etc. (You may also want to include wheat or graham crackers.)
2. Provide "spreads": cream cheese, peanut butter, or frostings.
3. Supply decorations: jelly beans, M & M's®, corn candy, thin licorice, tiny chocolate bits, Lifesavers®, gumdrops, nuts, yogurt drops, raisins, dried fruits, etc.

Wild Things Punch

1. Mix fruit punch with Sprite® and serve cold.
2. Or, serve fresh fruit juice.

The King of the Wild Things

© 1993 Mary Ellen Hicks (used by permission)

Verse 2:   I am the king of the wild things,
The beasts of the world all agree,
I send them off to bed with a nod of my head,
They always listen to me.
I am the king of the wild things,
But now all I think about is home.
My mom loves me the best, I'll forget about the rest,
Until the next time I want to roam,
Until the next time I want to roam.

Suggestions for Presenting Reader's Theater

Reader's Theater is an exciting and easy method of providing students with the opportunity to perform a play while minimizing the use of props, sets, costumes, or memorization. Students read the dialogue of the characters, narrator, chorus, etc., from a book or prepared script. The dialogue may be read verbatim from the book just as the author has written it, or an elaboration may be written by the performing students. Sound effects and dramatic voices can make these much like radio plays.

Everyone in the class can be involved in this presentation. There are ten speaking parts, the "Max was a Wild Thing" poem (page 18) can be read by six students, and the remainder of the class can sing the song, "The King of the Wild Things" (page 43).

1. The teacher may wish to construct the following "signs" out of sentence strips cut in half. Punch holes in the cards after laminating them and tie with yarn.

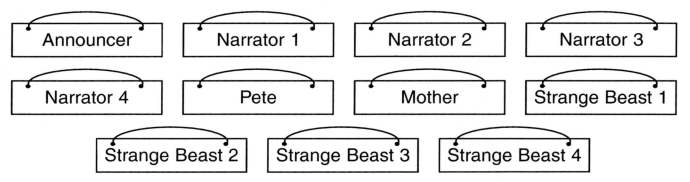

2. To present the poem (following the script), have six students come forward and hold up pictures they have created to go with the story or poem. The stanzas of the poem can be taped to the backs of the pictures. The students can display the pictures and read the stanzas of the poem in the correct order. (Be sure students do not cover up their faces with the pictures.)

3. If you are presenting the program to another class, the singers can stand off to one side in a group. If you are presenting the program in your own classroom, the singers are the audience, and, of course, the readers can also join in singing the song.

4. Sample arrangement of readers:

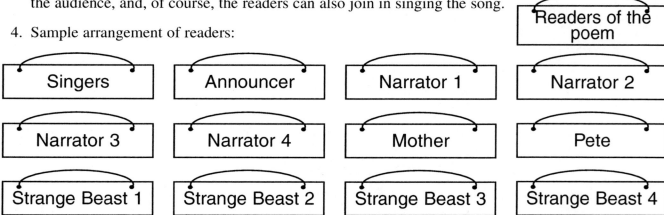

All the readers can walk "on stage" as they are introduced by the announcer and remain there throughout the program. The students who will read the poem can move to "center front" when they are ready to read, and the script characters can move off to one side.

Reader's Theater Script

Announcer: Welcome to our Reader's Theater presentation of *Where the Wild Things Are.* Our
readers are as follows:

Announcer –	Strange Beast 1 –
Narrator 1 –	Strange Beast 2 –
Narrator 2 –	Strange Beast 3 –
Narrator 3 –	Strange Beast 4 –
Narrator 4 –	
Pete –	
Mother –	

Narrator 1:   Pete just would not behave.

Narrator 2:   He did not want to take a bath before dinner.

Narrator 3:   He refused to clean up his messy room.

Narrator 4:   And he wouldn't stop teasing his little brother, Joey.

Mother: Stop teasing your brother, and go clean up your room...now!

Pete: No! It's fun to tease Joey, and I won't clean up my room!

Mother: You're acting like a strange little beast, not at all like my wonderful son, Pete.

Pete: I'm having fun! Grr...rr...rr! I'm a beast!

Mother *(angrily):*   That's it, Pete! You go up to your room right now and stay there all by yourself
until you can behave.

Narrator 1:   Pete did not want to go to his room.

Narrator 2:   He played for awhile, and then he lay down on his bed. The sun went down while
he slept.

Narrator 3:   Pete opened his eyes and looked up where his ceiling had once been. All he could
see was the sky overhead filled with stars.

Narrator 4:   Suddenly, a beautiful hot air balloon floated down into his room.

Narrator 1:   Pete jumped in, and off it flew over houses and rivers and mountains and forests.

Pete: This is great! I'm free! I'm never going back home!

Narrator 2:   Pete's balloon landed in a jungle far away.

Narrator 3:   He was met by four strange beasts who tried to scare him.

Strange Beast 1:   We're going to scare you, Pete. Grr...rr...rr!

Strange Beast 2:   Yes! Were going to howl and yell loudly.

Strange Beast 3:   And we're going to show you our ugly teeth and claws.

Strange Beast 4:   And we're going to make you mind us!

Pete: No! I came here to be free, and I'm in charge!

Narrator 4:   The strange beasts were very large, but they were just big babies.

Strange Beast 1:   Okay, you're the leader, Pete.

Strange Beast 2:   What do you want us to do, Pete?

Strange Beast 3:   Can we have a big parade, please Pete?

Reader's Theater Script *(cont.)*

Strange Beast 4:	Can we dance and have fun and eat lots of candy and cookies?
Pete:	Yes, to all of you! But you have to follow me!
Narrator 1:	They had a great time all night long.
Narrator 2:	But they made a very big mess.
Pete:	Stop! Everyone clean up this awful mess! Right now! And then all of you go take a bath!
Narrator 3:	Pete was tired of the strange beasts.
Narrator 4:	He missed his home and family.
Pete:	I'm going home. Goodbye!
Strange Beast 1:	Oh, no, Pete! We've never had such fun.
Strange Beast 2:	We'll miss you, Pete. Stay here.
Strange Beast 3:	Please stay with us forever!
Strange Beast 4:	Don't go, Pete! We love you!
Pete:	Sorry, I want to go home. So long to each of you!
Strange Beast 1:	Let's have another parade, Pete!
Strange Beast 2:	We'll follow you, Pete!
Strange Beast 3:	Look, Pete, I'm howling and yelling!
Strange Beast 4:	And I'm showing you my ugly teeth and claws!
Pete:	And I'm getting in my hot air balloon. Goodbye, strange beasts! I won't forget you! Goodbye!
Narrator 1:	Pete flew back home over forests and rivers and mountains and cities.
Narrator 2:	His mother was gently shaking him.
Mother:	Come on, Pete. I'll help you clean this room. Then we can go downstairs to dinner. Everyone's waiting for you.
Pete:	Okay, Mom. Thanks. Boy! I'm glad to be home.
Announcer:	We hope you enjoyed our story. We will now recite a poem (page 18) for you. The title is "Max Was a Wild Thing" by Susan Kilpatrick.
Announcer:	We will now sing a song (page 43) called "The King of the Wild Things" by M.E. Hicks.
Announcer:	This is the end of our program. Thank you for being such good listeners.

An Invitation to a Wild Rumpus

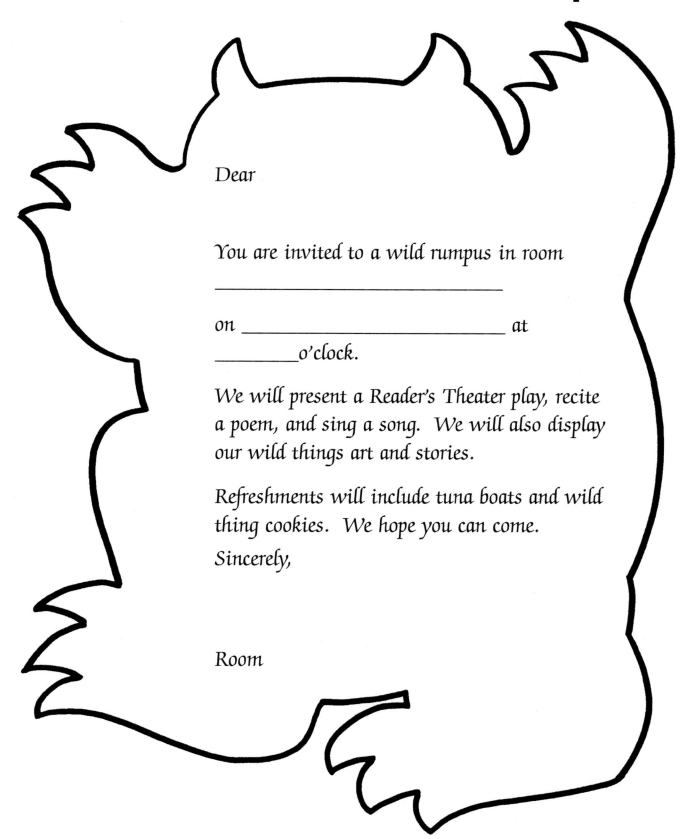

Dear

You are invited to a wild rumpus in room

_____

on _____ at

_____o'clock.

We will present a Reader's Theater play, recite a poem, and sing a song. We will also display our wild things art and stories.

Refreshments will include tuna boats and wild thing cookies. We hope you can come.
Sincerely,

Room

Bibliography

Related Literature

Brown, Ruth. *A Dark Tale.* (Dial, 1981)

Carrick, Carol. *Patrick's Dinosaur.* (Houghton, 1983)

Crowe, Robert L. *Clyde Monster.* (Dutton, 1976)

Delaney, M.C. *The Marigold Monster.* (Dutton, 1983)

Dinan, Carolyn. *The Lunch Box Monster.* (Faber Paper, 1983)

Dos Santos, Joyce Audy. *Henri and the Loup Garou.* (Pantheon, 1982)

Gackenbach, Dick. *Harry and the Terrible Whatzit.* (Houghton, 1978)

Garrison, Christian. *The Dream Eater.* (Macmillan, 1978)

Gruber, Suzanne. *Monster Under My Bed.* (Troll Assocs., 1985)

Hawkins, Colin. *Take Away Monsters.* (Putman, 1984)

Hutchins, Pat. *The Very Worst Monster.* (Greenwillow, 1985)

Issacsen-Bright, Margaret H. *Monster Don't Scare Me.* (Willowisp Pr., 1988)

Mayer, Mercer. *There's a Nightmare in My Closet.* (Dial, 1968)

Mayer, Mercer. *There's an Alligator Under My Bed.* (Dial, 1987)

Meddaugh, Susan. *Beast.* (Houghton, 1981)

Ross, Tony. *I'm Coming to Get You!* (Dial, 1984)

Stevenson, James. *What's Under My Bed?* (Greenwillow, 1982)

Willis, Jeanne. *Monster Bed.* (Lothrop, 1987)

Wylie, Joanne and David. *Do You Know Where Your Monster Is Tonight?* (Childrens, 1984)

Other Books by Maurice Sendak *(partial list)*

Higglety Pigglety Pop! Or There Must be More to Life. (HarpC Child Bks., 1979)

Kenny's Window. (HarpC Child Bks., 1989)

Seven Little Monsters. (HarpC Child Bks., 1977)

The Sign on Rosie's Door. (HarpC Child Bks., 1960)